FOR ||||||||||||| I

C000183840

A TIME
AS THIS

A pocket guide to the book of Esther

David Chapman

INTRODUCTION

The book of Esther is a fascinating story of how God preserved a large number of His Old Testament people from disaster.

The story plays out against a background of political intrigue and personal ambition.

The principal people reflect both admirable and dishonourable attitudes and actions.

In this short study guide the story is retold with reflective comments and questions to ponder.

Taken a section at a time it should take just a few days to complete the study but it is hoped that the lessons learned of God's providence and love for His people will remain with the reader for far longer.

OVERVIEW

Main themes

The book of Esther is one of only two books in the Bible named after women, the other being the book of Ruth. In this book we see the lives of several characters played out. There are some who are selfish and full of pride, seeking only personal position and power. There are those who risk everything for others, choosing integrity in the face of opposition. Esther is a book about developing godly character. In the midst of a culture that does not emphasize doing what is right, this book can speak to us profoundly. In this book we are given a description of what godly character is and what it is not.

The other main theme that underlies the story is that God is working in the circumstances and events of people's lives to bring about His plans. As God works in our lives we must choose to think and do what is right so that we can play a part in His plans.

The Jewish people were living in a predominantly Gentile society and so this book may help us to understand how we can live as Christians in a non-Christian society.

The book of Esther is annually read by Jewish people each year when they celebrate the Feast of Purim which is a feast instituted in the book (see 9:31). It is not, however, primarily a religious ceremony.

The role of the Jewish people in God's plan of salvation and the opposition they arouse because of their independence and difference from society underlie the story of Haman's desire to destroy them. God's unseen protecting hand ensures that the anti-Semitic hatred of His enemies will not ultimately triumph. Sadly at times anti-Semitism has been seen in the church even from such theological greats as Martin Luther who said of this book (and the apocryphal book of 2 Maccabees): *"I wish they did not exist at all; for they Judaize too much and have much heathen perverseness".*

The story of Esther points us to a Hidden Hand at work in the preservation of the Jews. It also provides an illustration and foreshadowing of the persecution of God's people down through history and their deliverance from it. This should be a great encouragement to all believers. G. Campbell Morgan states it strongly, saying, *"There is no situation in human life or experience for which a message of God cannot be found through the book."*

Setting

The events described in the book took place
in Persia during the reign of King Xerxes
(Ahasuerus in the KJV and NKJV). He reigned
from 486 BC to 465 BC. It is likely that the
events happened in 483 BC near the
beginning of his reign.

In the story of the Jews it is now 100 years
since the beginning of the exile in Babylon.
Persia has taken over the Babylonian empire
and in the aftermath many Jews have
returned to Jerusalem. The events of Esther
take place in the period between Ezra
chapters 6 and 7. There is a sixty year gap
between these chapters and Ezra led a
second group of exiles back to Jerusalem in
458 BC when Xerxes son Artaxerxes was
king of Persia.

The story takes place in the king's winter
residence of Susa rather than in Babylon. We
should note that the Persian Empire at this
time was vast, covering 127 provinces that
stretched from India to Ethiopia.

Principal Characters

Queen Vashti - the Queen of Persia as the
story begins. Her reluctance to meekly obey
the king in all things leads to her being
deposed. She refused to display herself at a
drunken party. Her modesty stands in

contrast to the behaviour of her husband King Xerxes. Her dismissal makes it possible for a new queen to be sought. We do not know what happened to Vashti after she was dismissed from the royal court.

King Xerxes - king of the vast Persian Empire. He was a sensual man who displayed a rashness in his judgements that had far reaching consequences.

Esther - an orphaned Jewish girl. Originally her name was Hadassah meaning *"myrtle"*. Her name was changed by the Persians to Esther meaning *"star"*, the name being a shortened form of the name of the Babylonian goddess Ishtar. She was a beautiful young woman who helped to save her people from genocide.

Mordecai - the uncle and guardian of Esther

Haman - the king's highest noble and adviser

It is perhaps notable that God is never mentioned in the book. No one is even recorded as mentioning as praying to God in the middle of the crisis (although prayer and fasting is mentioned). It is likely that this is a literary device by the author to underline the message of God's providence in the lives of men. The only other biblical book that does not mention God directly is the Song of Solomon.

Basic Outline

Danger for the Jews - chapters 1 - 5

> The prologue 1

> The king's first decree 2 - 3

> Haman's exasperation with Mordecai 4-5

A king who cannot sleep - chapter 6

Deliverance chapters - 6 - 9

> Mordecai's exaltation over Haman 6 - 7

> The king's second decree 8 - 9

Epilogue chapter 10

CHAPTER 1

Introduction

The story begins with an opening scene of a drunken party thrown by the powerful king of Persia. He is extravagantly entertaining leaders from around his vast empire of 127 provinces. The party continues for 180 days as he displays his great wealth.

Following this huge event Xerxes then holds another party. This time it only lasts seven days and was for those who were in the fortress in Susa. The banquet was for the men only. At the same time the Queen held a banquet for the women in the royal place. At the height of the revelry Xerxes commands that his queen, Vashti, should come so that he could show off her beauty to all the men present. The ancient Jewish Targum asserts that the king's command implied Vashti should appear *unveiled* before the other men, which would have been a disgrace in that culture. Her modesty, in the circumstances, was both commendable and daring.

The drunken Xerxes is furious with Vashti's response.

What should be done with Vashti?

Xerxes consults with seven advisers as to what he should do with Vashti now that she has publicly disobeyed him.

The leader of the advisers, Memucan, advises that Vashti has not only shown that she despises the king but that through her disobedience she will encourage every woman in the empire to disobey their husbands. To prevent this he tells the king to issue an irrevocable decree that will banish Vashti from the king's presence forever. By enacting this decree the message will go out loudly and clearly that women must always obey their husbands. He also tells Xerxes to choose another queen to replace Vashti. The king and his nobles thought this sounded a good idea and so on that very day he sent out decrees to every region in their own language to declare that every man should rule his home and should say whatever he pleases (*"what he says, goes"*, The Message).

Questions

1. Why might the king have given such an extravagant party?

2. The kings' request places Vashti in a difficult position. What factors would she have been weighing in her decision (v 12)?

3. Why did the advisers perceive Vashti's refusal to be dangerous to the kingdom?

CHAPTER 2

Introduction

In the first chapter of Esther we were introduced to the world of King Xerxes palace. We have seen the extravagance, the debauchery, the political intrigues and the making of unchangeable laws. Despite God not being mentioned we will see in this history of a pagan King and his court that God is preparing beforehand the circumstances whereby He will save His people.

A replacement for Queen Vashti

Chapter 2 begins with a sober and calm King Xerxes. He perhaps realised how rash he had been but he could not rescind the decree he had made against Queen Vashti. His attendants soon find a way to divert his attention. They suggest a huge beauty contest to supply the king with a number of young virgins to satisfy him. Throughout his vast empire there would be a search for young women to come to the court to be prepared to serve the king in his harem. Eventually the one who pleases him most would be crowned queen. The plan pleased the king. It pandered to his sensual nature and he would soon forget Vashti. She is never mentioned again.

Mordecai

We are now introduced to Mordecai who will play a crucial role in the story. He is a Jewish man from the tribe of Benjamin. He is a descendant of Kish who was an ancestor of King Saul and also a descendant of Shimei who was so loyal to Saul that he cursed David (2 Samuel 16:5). We are told that his family had been brought from Jerusalem to Babylon by King Nebuchadnezzar. We are not told how he now came to be in Susa.

Esther

Mordecai had a beautiful young cousin called Hadassah ("myrtle" in Hebrew), who becomes known as Esther (Persian for "star"). After her parents had died she was adopted by Mordecai who treated her like a daughter.

When the king's decree went out Esther together with many other young women from the empire were brought to King Xerxes fortress in Susa and added to his harem there.

Beauty treatment

The women were cared for by eunuchs and maids and underwent long periods of beauty treatments. These lasted at least 12 months (v12). Eventually Esther, along with others, was taken to the king's palace. When the king called for a woman she would be taken to him. She was able to choose the clothes and jewellery she would wear. If she pleased the king she would be added to his harem at the place.

Throughout this period of preparation Mordecai kept a watchful but distant eye on his cousin. At no time did Esther tell anyone of her nationality or family background (10).

Called to be Queen

In the seventh year of his reign King Xerxes called for Esther. This is four years after the banquets described in chapter 1. When Esther came to the king she pleased him greatly, more than any other. He quickly declared her to be the replacement for Vashti as queen and put the royal crown on her head. Typically he then declared a great banquet to celebrate.

Esther still did not tell anyone about her background and she continued to be advised by Mordecai who by now is a royal official.

A plot discovered

While Mordecai is working for the king he overhears a plot against him. He passed this information to Esther who told the king. The assassination plot was foiled and the incident was recorded in the king's history book. We are told that Mordecai was on duty "at the king's gate" which may indicate that he had a position as a magistrate. In ancient times legal disputes were often settled at the gates of a town or city.

Questions

1. Why was Mordecai's ancestry so important (5, 6)?

2. Why do you think Mordecai forbade Esther from mentioning her nationality?

3. Why did Mordecai sit at the king's gate?

CHAPTER 3

Haman

We now meet Haman. He is an Agagite, a descendant of King Agag, king of the Amalekites. He is an important official of the king. In fact he is promoted to be the chief of King Xerxes' officials. He is accorded respect by everyone because the king had commanded that this should be so. Normal protocol would have been that people bowed down to a high official as a matter of course. The fact that the king had to command it may indicate that there was a danger that people would not bow down to Haman because he was disliked. The king's commands should always be obeyed in the Persian Empire. Only one person did not obey the command, that person was Mordecai.

Mordecai

The other officials at the palace asked Mordecai why he didn't bow down to Haman. He refused to change his behaviour. At times Jews would bow down to government authorities as a sign of respect (see Genesis 23:7, 1 Samuel 24:8) but Mordecai did not want to bow down to a descendant of Israel's ancient enemies the Amalekites (see Deuteronomy 25:17). In all other respects he was a loyal servant of Xerxes but when his colleagues asked him why he did not bow to Haman his simple response was that he was a Jew. God is opposed to every generation of Amalekites and Mordecai is obedient to God. We have a descendant of King Saul pitted against a descendant of King Agag and Mordecai obeys God whereas Saul disobeyed (see 1 Samuel 15).

A plot hatched

When the other officials tell Haman about Mordecai's refusal to bow down before him he becomes very angry. His anger is not only directed at Mordecai but against all Jews. He loved to be revered and many Jews would not revere a mere man. His hatred for the Jews and his desire for political power drove him to concoct a plot against all of the Jews in the Persian Empire.

Five years after Esther has become queen Haman decides the time has come to take action against the Jews. He cast lots (*purim*) to decide when to destroy them. The date was set for nearly a year later. He had time now to devise and implement his plan. His hatred has gone beyond all reason, nothing but complete genocide would satisfy him.

Haman approached King Xerxes and accused the Jews of being disobedient to the king's law and of keeping themselves separate from other people. He tells the king it is in his interests to destroy them all. If the king agrees then Haman would donate a huge amount of money to the king's treasury. The king readily agreed to Haman's plan. He gave Haman his signet ring as a symbol of his authority and even said Haman could do as he pleased with the money and the people (11).

Haman dictated a decree to the royal secretaries that would be sent out to every noble and official throughout the empire. The decree was sealed with the king's signet ring. **It could never be revoked once issued**. The decree was swiftly delivered. All Jewish people of all ages would be killed on a single day about eleven months after the decree is signed. There is no opportunity for mercy, no exceptions. Whoever killed them would be rewarded by seizing their victims' property. After sending out the decree Haman and Xerxes sat down to drink. The chapter ends by saying that the people of Susa were confused. No doubt they couldn't understand why the king should take such drastic action against some of his own subjects.

Questions

1. Mordecai insists to Esther that she should keep her true identity hidden. Why do you think he did this?

2. Even though God has not been mentioned directly where do you see His hand moving in the story so far?

3. What do we learn about King Xerxes' character from chapter 3?

4. What do you think is the cause of Haman's intense reaction against Mordecai?

CHAPTER 4

Introduction

The decree to kill all the Jews in the Persian Empire has been sent out. The hatred that Haman had for the Jews, and especially Mordecai, and the weak character of King Xerxes has produced a situation of dire peril for God's people. From reading chapter 4 we will see that although the decree has been published throughout the empire its contents have not been made known within the royal harem at the King's palace.

This chapter is perhaps the best known in the book.

Mordecai's response to the decree (1-3)

When he hears the king's decree Mordecai reacts with actions indicating distress and mourning. Because he was in mourning clothes he was not allowed to enter the palace grounds so he stayed as close as he could. As the decree was distributed there was great mourning amongst the Jews throughout the empire. They mourned, fasted and put on sackcloth and ashes. At no point is prayer mentioned. Is this because there was none or because it was assumed that if you were fasting you would also be praying?

Esther's initial response (4 - 9)

It seems that Esther had not heard the decree. Her maids and eunuchs saw Mordecai in distress at the palace gates. When they told her she also became distressed, not because of the decree but because of her concern for Mordecai. She sent clothes for him to wear instead of the sackcloth he had put on. He refused to wear it. Esther then sent one of her attendants to find out from Mordecai what the problem was,

Mordecai explained the situation to the attendant and asked him to show Esther a copy of the decree. He then asked the attendant to ask Esther to go to the king to plead for mercy towards the Jews. The attendant obeyed Mordecai's request.

Esther's response to the decree and Mordecai's request (10 - 12)

When Esther sees the decree and hears Mordecai's request she quickly responds. The court protocol decreed that no one could approach the king unless they had been called for. To do so would risk an immediate death sentence. Although she had been proclaimed queen the same rule applied to Esther. King Xerxes had not called for her for 30 days and there was no knowing when he might. Esther gets the attendant to let Mordecai know that she could not just

approach the king with her request for
mercy.

Mordecai's challenge to Esther (13 - 14)

Mordecai's reply is probably the best known
part of the book. He warns Esther that being
in the palace will not protect her from the
decree. Presumably by now people knew that
she was related to Mordecai the Jew. He
also speaks of deliverance coming from
elsewhere for the Jews if she did not
intervene for them. This may be a reference
to his faith that God would deliver His people
or Mordecai may think that other political
leaders may intervene to oppose Haman's
plans. His final line to her was an inspiring
challenge, *"Who knows if perhaps you were
made queen for just such a time as this?"*
This challenge perhaps speaks of Mordecai's
belief in a providential God who oversees the
lives of His people.

His challenge can perhaps be summed up as:

- Face the reality!
- Don't sit on the fence!
- Seize the moment!

Esther rises to the challenge (15 - 17)

Mordecai's challenging words speak strongly
to Esther's heart. She calls upon Mordecai to
gather the Jews living in Susa to fast for

three days and nights for her. Again prayer is not mentioned, but perhaps can be assumed. She and her maids, who presumably were not all Jews, would also fast. At the end of the three days she would approach the king. If death would be her destiny she was prepared to risk her life for the sake of all her people. Under Haman's decree she was a dead woman walking anyway. Mordecai responded by obeying Esther's command.

Questions

1. Why did Mordecai tear his clothes (1 - 2)?

2. Couldn't a queen escape the king's edict (14)?

3. What evidence do you see in chapter 4 of Mordecai and Esther's faith?

CHAPTER 5

Esther's requests to the king (1 - 8)

On the third day Esther dressed in her royal finery and prepared to go to the king. She wisely does not show that she has been fasting or upset in any way. Before she enters the room he sees her in the next court room and held out his sceptre to call her into his presence. She showed humility by touching the end of the sceptre.

The king asks her what she wants before she has a chance to speak. He is obviously in a good mood (or being reckless!) because he says he will offer up to half his kingdom. Again we see the impulsive nature of King Xerxes, having not sent for Esther for over 30 days now he is prepared to give her up to half his kingdom.

Instead of outright pleading for the Jews in the open court where many would perhaps be watching she asks the king to come to a private banquet in his honour and to bring his friend Haman with him. She has seen how much the king enjoys banquets and being flattered! Immediately he calls for Haman to come and join him at Esther's banquet. Esther had previously arranged a banquet so they could go straight away, presumably as she and her maids fasted they

prepared, or had prepared for them, a
banquet.

At the banquet the king again asks Esther
what she really wants from him. Again rather
than tell him what she wants she asks him to
come to another banquet on the following
day and to bring Haman with him again.

Haman's hatred for Mordecai (9 - 14)

Haman's pride at being asked to a banquet
by Queen Esther makes him very happy. But
his happiness is cut short when he sees
Mordecai at the palace gate. Mordecai is still
refusing to bow down before him despite the
death decree. Haman fumes inside but
restrains his anger.

At home he gathered his family and friends
and bragged of all the honours he has
received. To crown all the honours is the fact
that the queen has invited him to dine with
her and the king alone for two days running.
However the pleasure and pride he got from
this was still not enough to satisfy him. The
mere sight of Mordecai sitting at the palace
gate infuriated him and stole his joy.

His wife and friends tell Haman to take action
to kill Mordecai, why wait until the decree is
put into effect. They encourage him to build
a high gallows (some versions call it a huge
impaling stake). They suggest that he kill

Mordecai on the next day before he goes to the banquet with Esther and Xerxes. He readily agrees to this and orders the preparations to be made.

Questions

1. Why do you think Esther waited for the second banquet to make her request (5:8)?

2. Why did Haman order such a high gallows (5:14)?

3. We are now half way through the book - what are the most important lessons you have learnt so far?

CHAPTER 6

King Xerxes' sleepless night (1 - 3)

While Haman is busy organising the building of the gallows to kill Mordecai, King Xerxes is having a sleepless night. He decides to have a book on the history of his reign read to him. Included in the account that was read was the story of how Mordecai had helped to foil the plot against the king that had been led by Bigthana and Teresh (see chapter 2:21-23). When the king heard this he asked if the man who had uncovered the plot had been rewarded for his loyalty. His attendants told him that nothing had been done to reward Mordecai.

The king and Haman (4 - 9)

As the king was hearing of Mordecai's loyalty Haman was on his way to ask the king to kill him. On hearing that Haman was in the outer court he ordered his attendants to bring him into his presence.

The king asked Haman for his advice as to how best to reward someone who had pleased him. Haman's only thought is that he must be the man that the King intended to honour. His pride is so strong that he cannot conceive of there being anyone who could also be honoured by the king. He suggests that the man should be honoured by being clothed in the king's royal robes and for him to be paraded in the streets riding one of the king's horses. In this way everyone in the city would be able to see how well the king rewarded those who please him. Doubtless he could already see in his mind's eye the spectacle that would unfold.

Haman's reaction to the king's decree (10 - 14)

The king is delighted by Haman's suggestion and instantly declares that everything Haman has described should be done to honour Mordecai. Haman has no choice but to obey the king. He put the royal robes on Mordecai, placed him on the king's horse and led him through the streets declaring *"This is what the king does for someone he wishes to honour!"* We can perhaps imagine the reaction of those who saw this. While Mordecai is being honoured, Haman is being humiliated. While Mordecai is being honoured the king's edict against the Jews are probably pinned to the trees of the city.

When Haman returns home he tells his wife and friends what has happened. Their reaction is interesting. Firstly, they still describe Mordecai as the man who has humiliated Haman when in fact it is the king's action and his own pride that has brought it upon him. Secondly, his wife says that as Mordecai is a Jew Haman's plans will never prosper against him. She warns that if he continues to oppose Mordecai it will be fatal, not for Mordecai but for him. His wife and friends are beginning to distance themselves from him. Their discussions are interrupted when the king's eunuchs arrive to escort Haman to Esther's planned banquet.

Questions

1. Why do you think that Mordecai's Jewish origin ensured Haman's downfall (13)?

2. Why had Mordecai not received a reward for saving the king's life?

CHAPTER 7

The tables are turned

The king and Haman arrive for Esther's second banquet. After beginning to drink wine the king again asks Esther what is the thing she wants to request of him. Esther boldly asks that the king spares her life and the lives of her people. She is succinct in her plea. It is not a long complicated speech. She tells him that they were all to be killed. She says that if they were to be enslaved she would not have brought her request as that would have just been a trivial matter. After all, as slaves they could have been productive workers for the king

Light begins to dawn in the king's mind. He seems to have finally realised that Esther is a Jew and that he had been persuaded to destroy even his own wife. He declares *"Who would be so presumptuous as to touch you?"* All the other Jews are not mentioned but Esther was his own wife and that made all the difference to the king.

Esther tells the king that it is Haman who has devised the plot. Haman does not protest but simply turns pale with fear. The king is so enraged that he leaves the room to walk in the palace garden. Doubtless his mind is in turmoil. He knows he cannot change the edict that he has issued. He knows he has been duped and persuaded by Haman to do something wicked. What would people think if one day he honoured Mordecai only to kill him afterwards? Who would ever trust him again? What would people think when they saw how Haman had deceived the king. They would think him to be weak, a fatal thing for a king!

Haman knows that the king is likely to order his death and so turns to Esther to plead for his life. He throws himself on Esther's couch just as the king re-enters the room. The king thinks that Haman is attacking Esther. The king's attendants enter and cover Haman's face. A death sentence has been pronounced without a word being spoken.

Harbana, one of the king's eunuchs, tells the king of the gallows that Haman has built to kill Mordecai, the man who had saved the king's life. The king orders that the gallows should be used to hang Haman instead.

When Haman is dead the king's anger subsided but the problem of saving Esther and the Jews has still not been resolved.

Questions

1. How has Haman's life been a picture of Jesus' words in Luke 14:11?

2. Why did Haman's advisers think Mordecai's Jewish origin ensured Haman's ruin?

3. What thoughts and emotions might the king and Haman experience when Esther presents her request (7:6 - 7)?

CHAPTER 8

Having dealt with Haman there was still the problem of his plot against the Jews. In this chapter we see the aftermath of Haman's downfall.

Haman's property and titles 1 – 2

Haman is now dead and the king gives his property to Esther. The king also calls for Mordecai to come to him. When he obediently comes the king gives Mordecai the signet ring that Haman had worn. This was a sign of authority. Esther then gives Mordecai charge over Haman's estate.

Esther pleads for her people 3 – 6

Haman may be dead but his plot against the Jews is still very much alive. The king's decree could not be simply revoked, not even the king could do that. Esther therefore implores the king to do something to save her people. It is an impassioned plea as she weeps before the king.

The king's response 7 – 8

The king responds positively to Esther's plea. He reminds her that he has already dealt with Haman and given his property over to her. He tells Esther and Mordecai that they could write a decree as they saw fit to deal with Haman's plot. He instructs them to seal this decree with his own signet ring which no one could then revoke. It seems that he now has complete trust in Esther and Mordecai. He doesn't even say that he would read it before it was sealed in his name.

The scribes do their work 9 – 10

The king's scribes are summoned and they wrote down exactly what Mordecai dictated to them. The decree was sealed with the king's signet ring and sent to all 127 provinces of the Persian Empire. It was written in every language of the Empire. It was sent to the rulers and governors of the provinces and to the Jews living throughout the Empire.

The decree's contents 11 -1 4

The decree stated that the Jews would be allowed to gather together to defend themselves when Haman's decree was enacted. They were authorised to destroy anyone who tried to attack them and to take their possessions. The king urged his couriers to act speedily to ensure that this new decree was in place before the day when Haman's decree would come into force.

Mordecai and the effect of the new decree 15 – 17

Mordecai is now clothed in royal robes and has a crown on his head in the presence of the king. He is greatly honoured in the city. The whole city of Susa rejoices (15). The Jewish population feels relief and joy as events have now unfolded. Throughout the Empire the Jews rejoice, have a holiday and hold feasts to celebrate. People even become Jews because many became fearful of the Jewish people (17).

Questions

1. Why did Esther still have to plead with the king?

2. Why couldn't the king change his own decrees?

CHAPTER 9

The Jews destroy their tormentors 1- 17

Finally the appointed day comes, the day when Haman's decree and Mordecai's decree both come into effect. Throughout the Empire the Jews rose up to destroy those who had hoped to destroy them. The leading officials and governors helped the Jews against their enemies. It is said that people had become fearful of Mordecai (3). Mordecai had become the greatest man in the Empire except for the king (4). His fame had spread far and wide.

The enemies of the Jews were killed and there were many of them. In Susa alone five hundred men were killed along with Haman's ten sons. When the king was told what had happened he wondered aloud how many more must have died across his lands if five hundred had been killed in one city. He asks Esther if she has a further request or petition. She replies that she would like the following day to be another day when the Jews could avenge themselves against their enemies and Haman's sons should be strung up from the gallows for all to see. The king grants her request and on the following day a further three hundred men are killed in Susa. On both days of slaughter the Jews did not take plunder from those they killed despite being allowed to by the decree. The same applied throughout the Empire. In all a total of seventy five thousand men were killed by the Jews over the two days.

The Feast of Purim 18 – 32

The celebration of their rescue from their enemies lasted for two days amongst the Jewish community. They feasted and they sent presents to one another and gifts for the poor (22). Queen Esther and Mordecai wrote a letter to institute an annual celebration of their deliverance. It was to be known as **Purim,** derived from the *"pur"* or *"lot"* that had been cast by Haman to decide the day when he sought to annihilate the Jews. This Jewish feast continues to this day and is held a month before Passover. The celebration of Purim involves both fasting and feasting and the giving of gifts.

Questions

1. How did Mordecai's edict provide for what Esther asked for in 8:5-6 without breaking the first edict?

2. Why might the Jews have left the plunder despite the king's permission to take it?

3. Why do you think the celebration of Purim is still so important to Jewish people?

CHAPTER 10

Mordecai's advancement

The book of Esther does not end with an account of Esther's subsequent life but tells instead of how Mordecai rose to the second highest rank in the Empire. It seems that he continued to work on behalf of his countrymen and was well regarded. We are told that His advancement was recorded in the history books of the kings of Media and Persia.

Questions

1. The book ends quite abruptly and the conclusion is more about Mordecai than Esther. Why do you think this is?

2. Looking back over the book how might you see the principles of Romans 8:28 being worked out?

Other books available by David Chapman from Amazon:

The Faithfulness of God – a daily devotional

Gospel Truth in Practice – a guide to Ephesians

Jesus Son of God Son of Man – a pocket guide to Mark's Gospel

All titles are available in paperback and Kindle editions.

More titles are in preparation.

David can be contacted by email at:

davec1862@outlook.com

Printed in Poland
by Amazon Fulfillment
Poland Sp. z o.o., Wrocław

57457557R00026